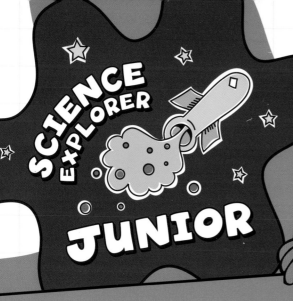

Think Like a Scientist on the Playground

by Dana Meachen Rau

CHERRY LAKE PUBLISHING · ANN ARBOR, MICHIGAN

CHERRY LAKE
Publishing

Published in the United States of America by Cherry Lake Publishing
Ann Arbor, Michigan
www.cherrylakepublishing.com

Content Editor: Robert Wolffe, EdD, Professor of Teacher Education,
Bradley University, Peoria, Illinois

The author would like to give a special thanks to Paula Meachen.

Design and Illustration: The Design Lab

Photo Credits: Page 1, ©zhuda/Shutterstock, Inc.; page 8, ©Laurence
Gough/Shutterstock, Inc.; page 11, ©Anthony Baggett/Dreamstime.
com; page 16, ©Georgios Kollidas/Dreamstime.com; page 17,
©Sportgraphic/Dreamstime.com; page 22, ©Mirmoor/Dreamstime.com;
page 23, ©The Art Gallery Collection/Alamy; page 28, ©Goh Siok
hian/Dreamstime.com; page 29, ©Jess Yu/Shutterstock, Inc

Library of Congress Cataloging-in-Publication Data
Rau, Dana Meachen, 1971–
  Think like a scientist on the playground/by Dana Meachen Rau.
     p. cm.—(Science explorer junior)
  Includes bibliographical references and index.
  ISBN-13: 978-1-61080-169-0 (lib. bdg.)
  ISBN-10: 1-61080-169-5 (lib. bdg.)
  1. Science—Methodology—Juvenile literature.
  2. Science—Experiments—Juvenile literature. I. Title.
  Q175.2.R38 2011
  501—dc22   2011010049

Cherry Lake Publishing would like to acknowledge the work
of The Partnership for 21st Century Skills. Please visit
www.21stcenturyskills.org for more information.

Printed in the United States of America
Corporate Graphics Inc.
July 2011
CLFA09

TABLE OF CONTENTS

How Does That Work?

Playground equipment can teach you a lot about science.

Have you ever looked at something and wondered, "How does that work?" Scientists do that all the time. Even on the playground.

You always slide down a slide, not up. Do you know why?

Science is at work when you zip down a slide, swing on the swings, play tag, and kick a ball. How long can you hang from the monkey bars? Why does your friend slide farther than you? How can you get your swing to go higher? You can use the science of **physics** to understand how and why things work the way they do.

STEP-BY-STEP

You can get your own answers by thinking like a scientist. Go step by step. You may have to repeat some steps as you go.

1. Observe what is going on.
2. Ask a question.
3. Guess the answer. This is called a **hypothesis**.
4. Design an **experiment** to test your idea.
5. Gather materials to test your idea.
6. Write down what happens.
7. Make a **conclusion**.

Don't forget your notepad!

Use words and numbers to write down what you've learned. It's okay if the experiment doesn't work. Try changing something, and then do the experiment again.

Take careful notes when you do experiments.

GET THE FACTS

Libraries have books, magazines, and computers that anyone can use.

Scientists look for facts before they start an experiment. They use this information as a place to start.

Where can you find information? A library is filled with books, magazines, and science videos

that can help you. You can ask a science teacher.
You can visit a museum with hands-on exhibits.

You can also find facts on the Internet. Be
careful. Not everything on the Internet is the truth.
Ask an adult to help you find the best places to
look for information.

Always put your safety first when using the Internet.

Hang On!

Some people can hold on to the monkey bars for a long time. Do you know why?

Time for recess! Try the monkey bars first. If you could reach the bars while still standing on the ground, you could probably hold on to them for a long time. But it's harder to hang on the bars when the ground is far below you. That's because of **gravity**.

The scientist Isaac Newton studied gravity. From his experiments, he concluded that all objects in the universe pull on each other. He also proved that the more **mass**, or matter, an object has, the greater its pull.

Isaac Newton was born in England in 1643.

Gravity is the **force** pulling you down to the ground when you're hanging on the monkey bars. Earth is pulling you toward its center. Your body is pulling on Earth, too. But Earth has more mass than you do, so its pull is stronger.

DO AN EXPERIMENT

How long can you and your friends hang on the monkey bars? In other words, how long can you resist the pull of gravity? Make a hypothesis. Then test it with an experiment.

A stopwatch will help you measure time accurately.

You'll need a stopwatch, a bunch of friends, and a set of monkey bars. You will also need a pencil and some paper. Start the watch when everyone starts hanging. Record the times as each person drops off. When the last person has finally let go, compare the times. Who dropped down first? Who stayed on the longest?

MAKE CONCLUSIONS

GRAVITY

Maybe you have some ideas about how you might hang on longer. Test them out.

It's hard to work against gravity! What helped some kids stay on longer? What made other kids drop off early? Were they wearing gloves? Did their hands get sweaty? **Weight** is a measure of how much Earth is pulling on you. Was everyone the same size? You may have noticed someone small and light was able to stay on longer.

Strength may have helped some kids stay on longer, too. Were some people in the group very athletic? If they have strong arms from pitching a baseball or playing tennis, their muscles helped them hang on.

Climbing on the monkey bars can make your arms stronger.

Rolling Along

Grab a ball and find an open area to play. If you kick a ball, it rolls for a while and then comes to a stop. Did you ever wonder why? The Italian scientist Galileo believed that a ball will keep rolling forever unless a force such as **friction** makes it stop.

Galileo was born in Italy in 1564.

Friction is the force that makes it harder for two objects to slide or roll past each other. When you roll a ball, there's friction between the ball and the ground. Do you think some materials create more friction than others?

There is friction between the soccer ball and the grass on this field.

Think about what you already know and then come up with a hypothesis.

Hypothesis: The ball will roll farther on pavement than on grass or sand.

Find a few flat areas on the playground with different surfaces, such as grass, pavement, and sand. Which surface will create the most friction with the ball? Make a guess.

To test this hypothesis, you'll need a playground, a ball, and a tape measure. You will also need a pencil and some paper to record your results. Place the ball on the grass. Push it to get it rolling. When it stops, measure the distance the ball rolled from your starting point.

Repeat these steps on the pavement and on the sand, using about the same amount of force to push the ball. Write down your results.

Did the ball travel the same distance on all three surfaces? Which surface had the most friction? Which one had the least? Why do you think this is? Why do you think the ball moved farther on some surfaces than others?

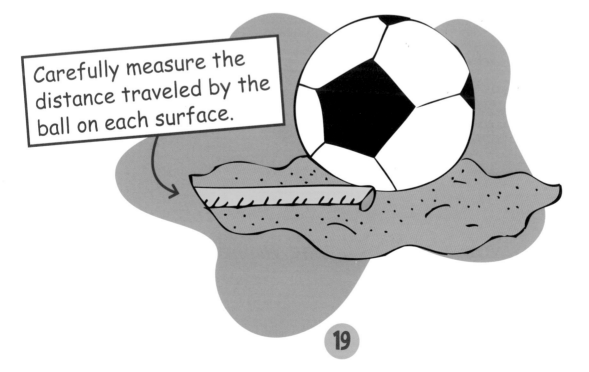

Carefully measure the distance traveled by the ball on each surface.

THINK FURTHER

You can use a slide to learn more about friction.

Galileo also experimented with balls and ramps. If he was at your playground, he would have the perfect ramp to use—the slide!

Just like the ball and the ground create friction, there is also friction between you and the slide when you slide down it. Take turns with your friends on the slide. Do some of you go down faster than others? Do you think that what you are wearing affects how easily you can slide down the slide?

Use what you know about friction to try to slide down the slide faster.

Get Energized!

You use a lot of energy when you play on the playground.

There's no doubt that the playground is full of **energy**. Kids run, jump, slide, swing, climb, and play. That's a lot of energy.

Work sounds like something you do in a classroom. But you're doing work on the playground, too. For scientists, energy means the ability to do work. Any time you use energy to make something move, you're doing work.

English scientist James Joule was born in 1818.

The scientist James Joule studied energy. Joule's experiments showed that energy can't be made or destroyed. Energy just changes from one form to another.

TRY AN EXPERIMENT

Hop on a swing. How can you get it to move? Do you flip a switch to turn it on? You need to do some work to get it swinging. But how? Test this hypothesis: You need to use your own energy to make a swing move.

Point your legs straight out in front of you while you lean back in the swing. Then lean forward and bend your legs back. Keep pumping this way, over and over again. Does the swing start to move?

You pump with your legs to make a swing move.

If you stop pumping your legs, the swing will slow down. Do you know why?

Your muscles use your energy to do the work to move the swing. Which way does the swing move when you pump your legs forward? Which way does it move when you pump your legs back? Why do you think this is? What happens when you pump harder?

When you are really high, stop pumping. Why does the swing move even when you've stopped doing work? Where is it getting its energy from?

Instead of pumping, have a friend push you instead. Who is doing the work now?

MAKE A CONCLUSION

Food is your body's source of energy.

You provide the energy to get the swing moving. But according to Joule, you didn't make that energy.

You had energy stored in your body. You got that energy from the sandwich you ate at lunch. The grains in the bread and the vegetables in that sandwich got their energy from the sun when they were growing.

Energy changes from one form to another. Thanks to the sun, you can swing on the swing!

The energy stored in fruits, vegetables, and grains comes from the sun.

Play and Discover

You can use a seesaw to experiment with balance.

Thinking, experimenting, and working aren't just for the classroom. You can do all these things on the playground, too! How do your conclusions about gravity, friction, and energy help you understand all the actions at recess?

Why it is easier to jump down than climb up?
Why are you all worn out after playing tag?
Where could you get some more energy?

Discover the answers next time you are on a playground. Think like a scientist everywhere you go!

Think like a scientist to come up with more questions to ask and answer on a playground.

GLOSSARY

conclusion (kuhn-KLOO-zhuhn) the answer or result of an experiment

energy (EN-ur-jee) the ability to do work

experiment (ik-SPER-uh-ment) a test of your idea

force (FORS) a push or pull that moves or affects an object

friction (FRIK-shuhn) the force that affects the way two objects move against each other

gravity (GRAV-i-tee) the pull or attraction of objects toward each other

hypothesis (hye-PAH-thi-sis) a guess

mass (MAS) the amount of matter in an object

physics (FIZ-iks) the science of matter and energy

weight (WATE) the measure of how much Earth's gravity is pulling on an object

FOR MORE INFORMATION

BOOKS

Green, Dan , and Simon Basher (illustrator). *Physics: Why Matter Matters!* New York: Kingfisher, 2008.

Hollihan, Kerrie Logan. *Isaac Newton and Physics for Kids.* Chicago: Chicago Review Press, 2009.

WEB SITES

Energy Quest

energyquest.ca.gov/index.html

Learn more about energy and some scientists who have answered big questions about it.

Exploratorium: The Museum of Science, Art, and Human Perception

www.exploratorium.edu/explore

Discover activities, exhibits, and videos that will help you learn more about all kinds of science topics.

INDEX

ABOUT THE AUTHOR

Dana Meachen Rau writes and experiments in Burlington, Connecticut. She has written more than 250 books for children.